Best wishes from all at Kennedy and Donkin
in York (and other friends too!)

Joe Cahill?? Doyle

Ian.

AFTER DISCOVERING COMES REDISCOVERING
ACCORDING TO "THE" BOOK. SOMETIMES,
SOME PLACE WE FEEL WE ARE BOUND
TO REDISCOVER M. B L.
LOOKING FORWARD TO IT FROM THE BOTTOM
OF OUR HEART,

Sonia & Carol Jan Royer

We'll miss you — + Rat Kat beer — so much
from ze eeenside! Hope to re-discover you soon
all love — Chris.

After reading the above
we thought- SINCLAIR was
hardware/software until we
discovered MAVIS!

WHO CAN MATCH YOUR DELECTABLE
BREW TO MIX WITH MY SUPERLATIVE BREW.
GUESS WHO? BUON VAYAGE Peter.
— Whatever the match it was delectable. Thanks for all your
help and cooperation. All the Best Richard Dorothy.
Good Luck Mattie in whatever you do.
South Shields, is not far away.

Howard Gill & Denny. XXX

Photograph page 3: Red Sea Coast at Khawkha

Photograph Title page: Mountains near Manakha

YEMEN
Rediscovered

Written and photographed

by Michael Jenner

Published in Association with
the Yemen Tourism Company

Longman

London and New York

Longman Group Limited
Longman House, Burnt Mill, Harlow,
Essex CM20 2JE, England
and Associated Companies throughout the world.

published in Association with the
Yemen Tourism Company,
P.O. Box 1526, Sana'a,
Yemen Arab Republic

First published 1983

ISBN 0 582 78359 3   English edition
      0 582 78358 5   French edition
      0 582 78357 7   German edition

British Library Cataloguing in Publication Data

Jenner, Michael
  Yemen rediscovered.
  1. Yemen
  I. Title
  953'.32 DS247.Y4

  ISBN 0-582-78359-3

British Library Cataloging in Publication Data
Jenner, Michael
  Yemen Rediscovered.
  Includes Index
  1. Yemen. 2. Yemen (People's Democratic Republic)
1. Yemen Tourism Company. II. Title
DS247.Y4J38 1983   953'.32 83-13537
ISBN 9-582-78359-3

Maps and diagrams by Swanston Graphics,
Derby, England.

Set in 12/16pt VIP Palatino
Printed in Great Britain by
William Clowes Ltd. Beccles and London.

Coast near Bir Ali

Mosque near Seyun

House in Hajjara

Islamic shrine in Wadi Hadramaut

Landscape of the Thula district

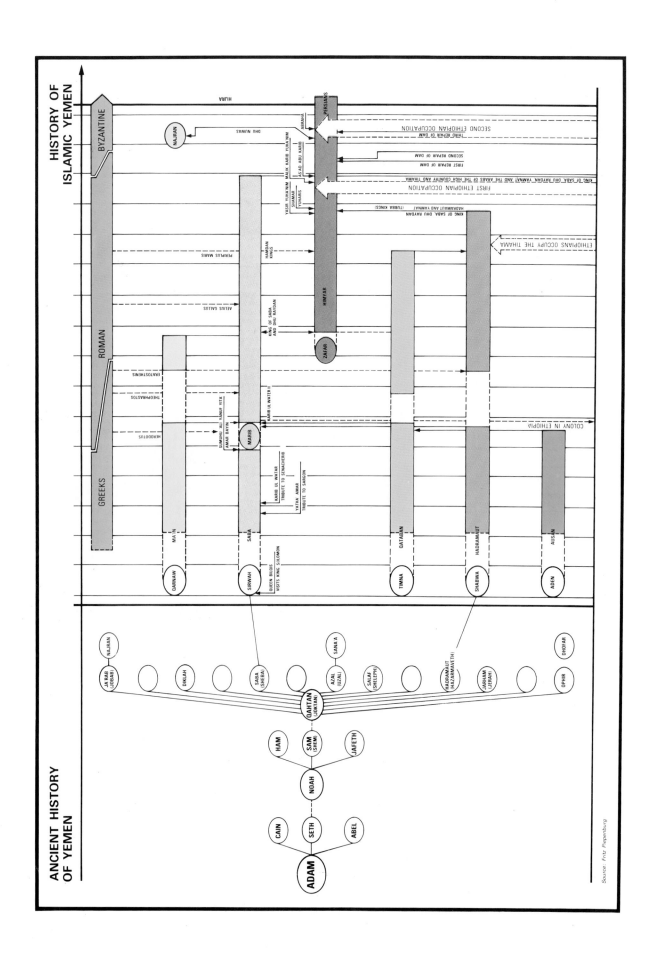

HISTORY OF ISLAMIC YEMEN

ANCIENT HISTORY OF YEMEN

Source: Fritz Piepenburg

14

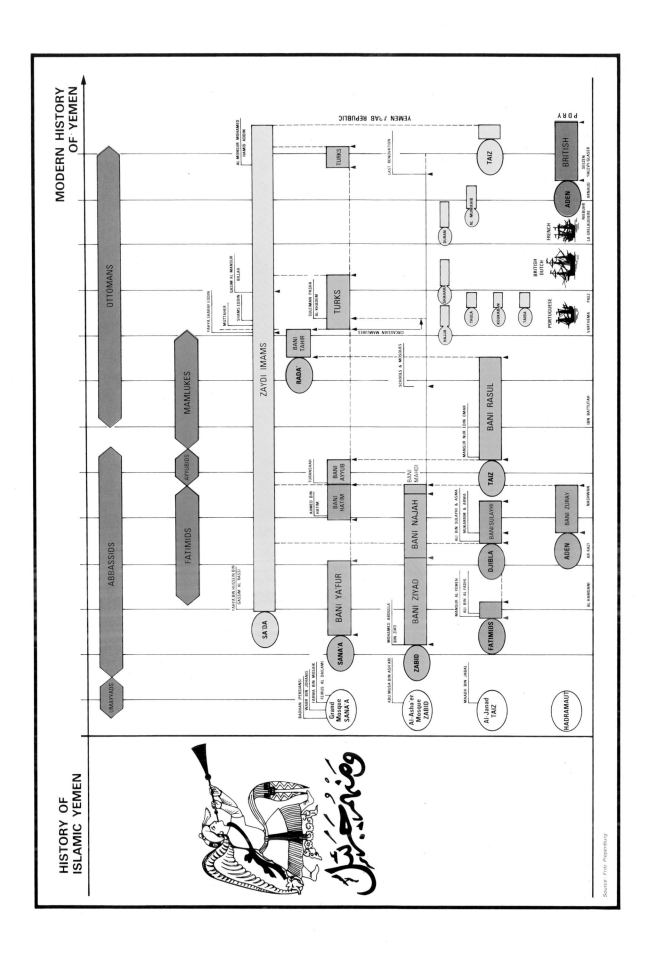

HISTORY OF
ISLAMIC YEMEN

MODERN HISTORY
OF YEMEN

15

South West Arabia, showing the main ancient trade routes

Source: This map is based on information supplied by Nigel St. J. Groom

Legend:
- Main sea routes for frankincense
- Secondary sea routes for frankincense
- Main overland frankincense route
- Secondary overland routes for frankincense

From India: Pepper, spices, sandalwood, ebony, precious stones, silk, ivory

To India: Cloth and clothing, frankincense, storax, glassware, metal and metal goods, wine, bullion

Frankincense and other aromatics, cassia, tortoiseshell, cinnamon and slaves from Horn of Africa. Aromatics, cinnabar and tortoiseshell from Socotra.

Frankincense in local boats from Moscha

Frankincense, aloes

Cloth and clothing, metalware, wine, corn, bullion, coral, perfume

Produce from India

Myrrh and other aromatics and cassia from Horn of Africa

Frankincense, myrrh and other aromatics

Cloth and clothing, metalware, tools and weapons, coral, corn

Ivory, tortoiseshell, rhinoceros horn, spices, coconuts from Azania (East Africa) to Muza

Myrrh, ivory, tortoiseshell

Cloth and clothing, corn, wine, saffron, glassware, storax, perfume, horses, bullion, olives, metalware, tools and weapons

Produce from India

Ivory, tortoiseshell, myrrh, slaves, cassia and cinnamon from Avalites to Muza and Ocelis

Myrrh, ivory

Ar-Rub 'Al-Khali (The Empty Quarter)

Ramlat Sabatayn (Sayhad)

Regions: MA'ĪN, SABA, HADRAMAUT, QATABĀN, AUSAN, HIMYAR

Places: Husn al-'Urr, Terim, Shibam, Madab, Mukalla, Bir Ali, Qana, Mayfa'at, Shabwa, Al-Bina, Habban, Al-'Abr, Nisab, Hagar an Nab, Tumna, Haribat, Marib, Sirwah, Na'd, Dhamar, Zafar (Sapphar), Am-'Adiyah, Nesca, Yatil (Baraquish), Ma'in, Sana'a, Shibam, Raydan, Sa'da, Nagran, Mesala, Taiz, Sawa (Save), Mokha (Al-Mukha), Muza, Ocelis, 'Adan (Eudaemon Arabia), Assab

Gulf of Aden

Red Sea

Kilometres 0 20 40 60 80 100 120

N

Contents

List of Plates

Acknowledgements

The author would like to thank Professor A. F. L. Beeston of the University of Oxford, Dr Yusuf Mohammed Abdullah of the University of Sana'a and Dr Sultan Naji of the University of Aden for their advice and comments on the text. Any errors in fact or judgement are nevertheless the responsibility of the author alone.

The support and assistance of the authorities in Yemen, and especially of the Yemen Tourism Company and Yemenia have been invaluable in the preparation of this work.

Thanks for research material and facilities are also due to the British Museum and to the School of Oriental and African Studies in London. Nigel St John Groom has been extremely helpful in preparing the map of South West Arabia, on page 16 and Fritz Piepenburg devised the historical charts on pages 14 and 15.

Finally, the generous co-operation of so many people in Yemen has made the field research and photography a truly rewarding experience. It is to the people of Yemen that this book is dedicated.

Preface

Until recently Yemen was considered one of the most mysterious countries in the world. The present northern part of the country, the Yemen Arab Republic, was practically closed to foreigners until the 1962 Revolution which ended the rule of Imamate. Much of the southern part of the country – with the exception of Aden, which was a British colony – had for long been difficult of access due to the fiercely defended autonomy of some of the tribes. Now the People's Democratic Republic of Yemen has taken steps to bring the vast hinterland within the apparatus of socialist administration.

More recently, the co-operation between the Yemen Arab Republic and the People's Democratic Republic of Yemen has matured into a positive policy to encourage tourism. To that end the Yemen Tourism Company was founded by the governments of both countries so that visitors may now view the culture of Yemen as a whole.

Although there are today two Yemen States, the cultural heritage of Yemen must be regarded as one. The ancient kingdoms of the incense trade, Saba, Ma'in, Qataban, Ausan, Hadramaut, and Himyar, which flourished from before 800 BC to AD 500, straddled the whole of south Arabia. This was a rich and sophisticated civilisation, which played a pre-eminent role in the great trade movement between the Far East, India and Egypt, Babylon, Greece, Rome and Byzantium in their respective periods. The abandoned cities of Baraqish, Marib, Timna and Shabwa still offer much scope for archaeological investigation.

Chapter One aims to outline the growth of the ancient kingdoms and to trace their eventual decline. Chapter Two describes the rise of Islam in Yemen from the 7th century to the middle of the 15th when the country found itself once more at the centre of world events, and a part of the Islamic Empire. Chapter Three takes the story of Yemen into the modern age but without delving into the contemporary reality of economic development plans and socio-political change. Chapter Four charts the gradual progress of the explorers, braving considerable dangers and natural obstacles, who greatly added to knowledge of Yemen in the outside world. Chapter Five describes travel facilities in Yemen. The introduction serves as a pen portrait of the making of the Yemeni landscape with its distinctive villages and cities. The colour photographs have been grouped geographically to show the diversity of Yemen's physical aspects.

Yemen Rediscovered does not attempt to be a guide book or an academic treatise but to provide an historical and cultural introduction to one of the least known but most significant civilisations of the Middle East.

Introduction

The Land, its People, and their Habitat

Yemen is more than just the southern extremity of the great land mass of Arabia. The climate, topography, and even some ethnic features distinguish Yemen from the country to the north. This identity has been reinforced by geographic remoteness to create over the millennia a distinctive political and cultural entity which, although now an integral part of the Arab world and of the Islamic community, yet has roots in a much more distant antiquity.

The ruggedness of the mountain terrain sets Yemen apart from the desert wastes which occupy most of Arabia. Walter Harris recorded with some surprise the landscape he encountered on his visit to Yemen in 1892: "...rich green valleys, well timbered in places, and threaded by silvery streams of dancing water; sloping fields gay with crops and wild-flowers; terraced or jungle-covered slopes." The mountains of Yemen reach a height of over 3,000 metres and form the backbone of the country, determining its climate.

The central highlands are high enough to catch the limited rainfall carried by the wind. Especially in April and August, the south west summer monsoons deposit enough precipitation to create the "rich green valleys" of which Harris wrote. The winter season, usually from November to February, is relatively dry as the prevailing wind is from the Central Asian Anticyclone. Yet even during the summer the rainfall is sporadic, often coming in thunderstorms, and extremely localised. Yemen's rainfall, although in the Arabian context a great blessing, thus presents a considerable challenge to the ingenuity of the farmers.

The mountainous terrain and the unpredictability of the rain have been the two shaping factors in the physical appearance of the Yemeni landscape. Niebuhr, sole survivor of the Danish expedition in 1762/4, observed: "The hills which they occupy are high and precipitous, yet cultivated up to their loftiest peaks, and abounding in productions of various sorts." The cultivation was made possible by mountain terracing. The last available scrap of land was carved from the mountainside and supported by a dry stone wall. This prevented not only erosion of the soil but also loss of the surface water, which would otherwise have run away into the valley. The terraces of the central highlands which extend from Sana'a in the north down to Ibb and Taiz in the south are the remarkable work of generations of farmer-builders, the landscape artists of Yemen.

The origins of the mountain terraces are remote. Possibly they date from Sabaean times but doubtless they flourished during the aftermath of the ancient kingdoms. At this time the extensive fields which depended on vast hydrological works such as the dam at Marib were progressively abandoned. Many of the agriculturalists drifted west and resettled in the mountains and set about transforming the rocky slopes into fields. The labour required to accomplish the task must have been colossal – as was the social organisation both within the tribe and between the tribes.

The village community is the basic unit of the social structure in both ancient and modern Yemen. It is the invisible architect of the mountain settlements which are in such harmony with their harsh surroundings. This sense of belonging among the rugged peaks of the highlands stems from the entire community. "Yemeni people feel secure in the mountains. They understand them. They know how to live with them and use them", writes Dr Yusuf Mohammed Abdullah, of the University of Sana'a. The relationship is instinctive and collective. It is rare to see isolated houses in the mountains of Yemen; instead, the village dominates the scene.

The village is more than an assemblage of individual family houses. There is an overall concept, the need for defence, which sets the ground rules of the planning. The mountain hamlets are built as fortresses with the houses themselves forming the walls. Thus huddled together they present the outside world with a stout rampart against unwelcome intruders. The same idea in action is to be found all over Yemen, from the mountains of the north to the great Wadi Hadramaut in the south, where the town of Shibam rises from the valley as one cohesive structure, eight to nine storeys in height. It is a solid defensive mass of mud building when viewed from a distance but on closer inspection it reveals itself as a community of separate dwellings.

Thus there is a unity of concept in the lay-out of hamlet and village but there is a great diversity in their form and decoration. The total reliance on local materials has resulted in a homogeneous quality. The stone structures of the mountains in the north and the mud-brick towers of the valleys in the south appear as continuations of the ground on which they stand. It is often impossible to know where the rock or cliff stops and the village begins. A group of houses can be mistaken for an out-crop of the land itself.

The cities of Yemen are as diverse in style as the villages and hamlets. The urban tradition is assumed to go back to the

Sabaean, Minaean and Himyaritic civilisations, yet the labyrinthine pattern of Yemen's principal cities demonstrates the same organic structure, unplanned and yet functional, which is characteristic of the Islamic tradition throughout the Middle East.

The unique contribution of Yemen to the city is both conceptual and architectural. The houses are terraced and, unlike the traditional Arab home which is constructed around a courtyard and looks in on itself, the houses look outwards. In Sana'a the best reception room, the *mafraj*, is at the very top, with windows on all sides affording panoramic views. The Yemeni love of external decoration is also contrary to the norm in Arabia, where usually the houses – apart from their ornate front doors – present the passer-by with a series of blank walls.

In Yemen the houses are not just modules or housing units in the urban jigsaw but works of design in their own right. In Zabid the brickwork is used to create monochrome patterns, in Sana'a limewash around the windows gives each house individual character within the overall concept; and in Sa'da it is the construction technique of superimposing layers of mud which creates the design of the house. The authors of *Yemen — Land of Builders* described Sa'da as "halfway between architecture and sculpture". That applies quite generally to urban settlements in Yemen.

As one travels through the regions of Yemen, from the hot coastal plain of the Tihama to the cool mountain villages of the central highlands and to the remote valleys of the Hadramaut there is such a diversity of landscape, architecture, and vegetation that it is like moving from one country to another. Yet the impression of Yemen as a land of contrasts is deceptive. There are common strands of identity running through the fabric. The fiercely individualistic character of each place and its people reveals itself gradually not as a discordant factor in essence but as the way of the country as a whole. The common identity of Yemen does not exist necessarily in a sense of uniformity or consensus of opinion but rather in the vigorous defence of the small unit, be it family or tribe or village. A unified cultural heritage underlies the diversity of expression.

The Ancient History of Yemen

Conventionalised face from a funerary stela of alabaster, 3rd-2nd century BC

South Arabia (or Yemen) is scarcely mentioned in the histories of the ancient civilisations of the Middle East. Writers pass directly from the wonders of Pharaonic Egypt and Babylon to the familiar world of the Greeks and Romans. Yet South Arabia played a crucial role in the economic development of the Middle East and, for a period spanning at least 1,300 years from before 800 BC to the 6th century AD, there flourished in that part of Arabia now known as Yemen a number of kingdoms which attained a level of prosperity and technological achievement comparable to that of the empires in the north at the same time.

A few of these kingdoms are known only to specialists and archaeologists, so that the once distinct kingdoms of Ma'in, Saba, Qataban, Ausan, Hadramaut and Himyar are generally referred to as pre-Islamic civilisation in south Arabia. This is partly due to the fact that Islamic historians have traditionally taken the birth of the Prophet as the starting point in their enquiries into the past and they transmitted mainly the memory of Himyar which had declined some decades before Islam. The epic story of those kingdoms, however, was narrated and has remained alive to the present day.

A more immediate reason for the oblivion into which the ancient kingdoms of Yemen have fallen is, to some extent, their geographic remoteness from today's centres of population. The sites of the abandoned capital cities are situated on the desert fringe of Yemen's eastern frontier with the Empty Quarter. In regions which once supported thousands there are today merely hundreds leading a semi-nomadic marginal existence. Furthermore, the ancient kingdoms of Yemen did not develop into empires. Their traces remained limited. Yemen's long withdrawal into isolation made a final contribution to the ignorance surrounding the past.

It was not until the 19th century that the first learned men and travellers managed to penetrate the forbidding interior of Yemen, often at great personal risk, to begin the task of documenting the archaeological sites. Some remained inaccessible well into the 20th century. Shabwa, the original capital of the Kingdom of Hadramaut, became the goal of a series of explorers, romantics and academics in the 1930s. H. St. John Philby visited Shabwa in 1936 and found the ruins "poor and vicious and mean ... disappointingly small and insignificant". Recent excavations by a French expedition are now revealing the full extent of Shabwa's former glory, and the available evidence confirms the city's dominant role in the economic activity which laid the foundation of south Arabia's early prosperity: the trade in incense and aromatics.

The use of frankincense and myrrh for mummification and religious rites is first associated with Pharaonic Egypt and Babylon, but the aromatic gums were precious commodities throughout the ancient world. Their uses extended from medicine and cosmetics to food flavouring and chewing gum. The Egyptians' search for a regular supply in the "Land of Punt" possibly took them to the incense producing areas in Arabia, located in Hadramaut and Dhofar. However, the sea route was not yet quite practical. The domestication of the camel and its use as a beast of burden much facilitated the south Arabian incense trade. The camel's domestication is believed to pre-date the first millennium BC but there is no evidence to suggest the incense trade from south Arabia was significant before 1000 BC. However, in the Greek and Roman periods south Arabia emerged as the principal source of supply of frankincense and myrrh, as well as many other luxury commodities, to the imperial courts and sophisticated cities to the north. It was the camel caravans plying the incense route which provided the economic stimulus to the flourishing of a string of kingdoms and cities which stretched from the seaport of Qana at the Arabian Sea in the south, through Shabwa, Marib, Nagran, Dedan, Petra to the seaport Gaza on the Mediterranean in the north.

A sedentary civilisation based on agriculture through efficient irrigation methods predated the incense trade. It is assumed that communities existing on the fringe of the Sarat mountain chain and hemmed in by the desert found themselves strategically located to become way stations on the incense route. Thus it was that the edge of the Empty Quarter became the main artery of a booming trade for over a thousand years.

The organisation of the commerce along the route was highly sophisticated. Although the tribal kingdoms were intermittently at war throughout the period of their prosperity, they were all economically interdependent and co-operated to channel the flow of caravans from one to the other. Each took a commission from the merchants in return for that protection which is the key to safe passage through tribal territories in the desert. Yet it must be stressed that the need for protection stemmed not only from the threat of undisciplined marauders but also from looting and attack on the part of the "protectors" themselves. From Pliny's account of the incense trade at Shabwa we learn that the penalty for deviating from the prescribed route was severe: death.

The following passage from Pliny's *Natural History* shows the degree of commercial oganisation attained: "Frankincense after being collected is conveyed to Sabota (Shabwa) on camels, one of the gates of the city being opened for its admission; the kings have made it a capital offence for camels so laden to turn aside from the high road. At Sabota a tithe estimated by measure and not by weight is taken by the priests for the god they call Sabin, and the incense is not allowed to be put on the market until this has been done; this tithe is drawn on to defray what is a public expenditure, for actually on a fixed number of days the god graciously entertains guests at a banquet. It can be exported by the Gebbanitae (Qatabanians) and accordingly a tax is paid on it to the king of that people as well.

"Their capital is Thomna (Timna) which is 1487½ miles distant from the town of Gaza on the Mediterranean coast; the journey is divided into 65 stages with halts for camels." (Bk. 12, ch 32, secs 63-4).

In addition to Sabota (Shabwa) described above by Pliny, the main cities of the ancient kingdoms were Timna in Qataban, Marib in Saba, and Baraqish and Qarnaw in Ma'in. It is largely from the archaeological evidence from these sites that a picture of the life in these city states is being pieced together. A comprehensive view of the social life of the time is yet to emerge but it is known that there was a surprising diversity of administration ranging from kings to consultative councils. Polytheism was the common practice and the temples were dedicated mainly to astral deities representing the sun and the moon and the morning star. There was a strong belief in the after-life as witnessed by the burial of personal possessions with the dead.

Examples of early south Arabian art on display in the National Museum in Sana'a and the National Archaeological Museum in Aden provide the most intriguing expression of the cultural climate. One can witness the gradual development of sculpture from stylised bas relief to three-dimensional figures with individual features. Greek and Roman influence permeated back down the incense trail and dictated the changes. The most authentic south Arabian pieces are the small standing figures of marble or alabaster. The bodies are shortened to focus attention on the mask-like faces so that the general impression is of sad, impassive and oversized chessmen. The architectural decoration progresses from simple geometric design to more fanciful floral patterns, which might indicate a shift from austerity to luxury as the revenues from the incense trade multiplied. The neatly-incised geometric characters of the inscriptions are in harmony with the form of the buildings; the temples being usually of rectangular plan with square columns. The original style of the early period surpasses in creativity those later works which bear the influence of Hellenistic culture.

Alabaster slab 4th-3rd century BC. *Dedication by Ri'ab and his family*

South Arabian kingdoms did not succeed one another in ruling over the region, but were all almost contemporaneous although they reached their peak at different times. Himyar, however, was the last, and Saba encompassed the entire period so that the term Sabaean is sometimes used to denote the whole civilisation. In addition, there were shifting coalitions and wars as the individual kingdoms vied for power in the tradition of tribal federations. Towards the end of the incense kingdoms, the Himyaritic challenge to Saba was so strong that in the last quarter of the third century AD a Himyarite assumed the title of King of Saba, Dhu Raydan, Hadramaut, and Yamnat; a century later the title of the king comprised also the Bedouins in the highlands and the lowlands. This period of history marked the first political unification of all south Arabia under a single ruler. Accordingly the term Himyaritic is used alongside Sabaean as a general epithet for pre-Islamic civilisation in Yemen.

Saba was nonetheless the most dominant over more than a thousand years and its political vision created a society beyond the limits of the tribe. The neighbouring kingdom to the north, Ma'in, appears consistently in the role of incense traders. There were Minaean business communities in each of the capital cities of the other kingdoms and they provided much of the organisation and commercial expertise. Minaean influence extended northwards as far as Petra; accounts of this Nabataean city always portray the bearers of incense from south Arabia as Minaeans, who maintained trading links with several countries around the Mediterranean. Yet, of the ancient kingdoms only Hadramaut was a producer and it relied to a considerable extent on the region of Dhofar for supplies of frankincense which were transported by sea to the port of Qana (today Bir Ali) for the overland journey north via Shabwa.

The consumers at the end of the incense road did not receive much precise information about the origin of the commodities purchased so dearly. The cultivation of the frankincense tree was surrounded by mystery. Herodotus writes of winged serpents guarding the groves which were tended by a select body of men not permitted to touch women or to witness funeral processions. Outside knowledge of the incense trade was so scanty that one cannot help wondering if the Minaean merchants and others conspired to deceive in order to protect their monopoly.

This seems likely in view of the fact that the ancient Yemenites had other secrets of commercial importance to conceal. They had also mastered the monsoon winds – and kept it a secret – which made trade by sea with India and China a practical venture. The incense route thus served to transport other luxury goods much in demand such as silk and spices which were landed at ports along the coast of south Arabia for the overland trek by camel caravan. For centuries the Greeks and Romans believed that the kingdoms of south Arabia produced all the luxuries of the Orient, hence the Roman description of Yemen as *Arabia Felix* or ''Fortunate Arabia''.

Part of the myth of fantastic riches in south Arabia can be ascribed to the high prices paid for frankincense and myrrh. These were, however, in relation to the dangers and rigours of the 2735-kilometre journey the length of the Arabian peninsula, and the revenue from the incense trade was distributed all along the route. It would appear that – as with the oil income of today's Arabia – the majority of the population was not relieved of the necessity of labour. In any case the production of food and the irrigation works needed to sustain agriculture in such arid terrain must have consumed the energies of thousands of workers in each of the major centres. Thus the Roman image of *Arabia Felix* has to be set against the probable reality of unremitting toil in a difficult environment. The impressive hydrological works such as the famous dam at Marib convey a real feeling of the basis of the old civilisations.

It is important to note that the dams of the ancient kingdoms of Yemen did not rely on water from perennial rivers to form a reservoir system; instead the dams were constructed to deflect the run-off from occasional rain into irrigation canals. What remains at Marib are the imposing sluices on each side of the wadi. The huge blocks of masonry bear witness to the skill and diligence of the Sabaeans. It is estimated that the fields irrigated by this dam extended to more than 1600 hectares and could have provided food for 300,000 people. Traces of the old fields are still to be seen. There is a project to build a new dam higher up, in order to restore the agricultural potential of the area. A new tarmac road has been built to improve communications to the city of Sana'a, and Marib awaits its renaissance.

In the popular imagination Marib is inextricably linked with the legendary visit of the Queen of Sheba (Saba) to the court of King Solomon in Palestine. Although this visit is recorded in both the Old Testament (10 Kings: 1-13 and 9 Chronicles: 1-12) and the Qur'an (Sura 27 *al Naml* and Sura 34 *Saba*) there is considerable divergence of opinion concerning the circumstances of the visit. The more colourful story has Bilqis, Queen of Sheba, drawn by the wisdom of Solomon, journeying from Marib in a vast caravan and concluding trade agreements as well as entering into intimate relations with Solomon. There is a more prosaic version, according to which Sheba was merely a northern branch of the Saba tribe, living close to Solomon's kingdom. Neither the references in the Qur'an nor those in the Bible to the

Queen of Sheba, give her name. It is hoped that further excavation at Marib will yield conclusive evidence of the Bilqis legend.

Alabaster head c. 4th century BC

The legend which surrounds the story of the Queen of Sheba serves the more practical purpose of focusing attention on the importance of the Yemeni cultural heritage. Until recent times the archaeological value of Marib and other sites was not adequately recognised by the local populations. There was much wanton destruction of the ruins by the practice of using stones from the Sabaean sites for the construction of new houses. A fresh awareness of the importance of Yemen's pre-Islamic past is leading to better protection of the sites and to more professional archaeological digs.

The sites still have many secrets to yield but one of the greatest riddles is that most are located in what are today almost waterless, inhospitable regions. The early accounts of the incense route leading entirely through rich agricultural regions are probably based on imagination rather than fact. Certainly the irrigation schemes would have made a great contribution to the greening of the desert and there is a growing body of opinion that there could have been a substantial change in climatic conditions over the past 3,000 years. Research programmes have yet to reveal the actual extent of the old civilisations.

Marib serves both as a symbol of the decline as well as of the splendour of the ancient kingdoms. The collapse of the dam in the 5th century, its subsequent repair and final collapse in the second half of the 6th century, are often taken as landmarks in the demise of Sabaean civilisation. Yet the important point is not the collapse of the dam but that the means or the motivation to rebuild it were ultimately lacking. One of the causes for the abandonment of the dam was the changing economic situation which from the 4th century onwards had become acute enough to threaten the viability of the incense route on which the prosperity of the civilisation depended.

Firstly, the discovery of the direct sea route to India by the Romans using the monsoon winds challenged south Arabia's role as commercial middleman between the Mediterranean, India and the Orient. The increasing economic instability of the Roman Empire had depressed the market for incense. The transfer of power to Constantinople in 395 gave prosperity to the silk route for the Indian and Chinese trade via Persia to the capital of the eastern Roman Empire. Finally, the spread of Christianity under Byzantium in the 4th and 5th centuries had a substantial impact on Roman religious rites, such as cremation, which had required such vast quantities of incense.

There was a general fall-off in economic activity as the entire civilisation changed gear. The kingdoms which had formed into highly sophisticated tribal centres were but pockets of developed culture in a region still characterised by anarchy and nomadic lifestyle. With the decline in wealth there was a drift away from the once prosperous centres and a progressive bedouinisation of society ensued. Eventually neither the money nor the skills nor sufficient people were available to maintain the hydrological works and much fertile land was gradually reclaimed by the desert. A cultural fatigue lay over the old political structure of Yemen; a natural accompaniment to the material decline after the years of plenty.

From the 4th century AD polytheism had been facing a sturdy challenge from the principle of monotheism, widely current in the contemporary Hellenistic world with its rivalries between on the one hand ancient polytheism and on the other hand Christianity, Judaism and other monotheistic cults. The last king of the Himyarites, Dhu Nawas, converted to Judaism and, through his persecution of the Christians at Najran, brought on himself a Christian invasion from Ethiopia in 518 or 523. There is record of major repairs to the dam at Marib in 543 before it was finally abandoned some twenty to thirty years later. The original energy of Saba was evidently exhausted, and it is likely that the end of the ancient kingdom was due as much to cultural collapse as to physical disaster.

Thus more than one thousand years of developed civilisation came to an end. The very settlements were abandoned as the people drifted off either into a primitive nomadic existence or trekked into the mountains to carve small fields out of the slopes by the use of stone terracing. The glory that was Ma'in, Qataban, Ausan, and Hadramaut, and above that Saba and Himyar, faded in the collective memory. The incense route was forgotten. With the introduction of Arabic even the Himyaritic inscriptions had become meaningless within a hundred years. The incense tree became a rarity due to neglect of organised cultivation. The irrigation schemes fell into disuse and the fields returned to desert sand.

However, the ancient civilisation of Yemen has survived in less obvious ways. The building skills have been handed down to the present day. Yemeni craftsmen still construct the most daring of stone edifices without resort to mortar or measuring tools. The irrigation skills live on in the mountain terracing. The tribal tradition and the application of customary law have managed to remain side by side with Islamic *sharia*, and the market regulations found at Timna dating from the 4th century BC could still be applied almost unchanged. The theocratic tradition which began with the early kingdoms – although power was later secularised – could still be seen in some respect until 1962 in the institution of the Imamate. The Imams used red ink on official proclamations, a practice which may be traced back to the kingdom of Himyar. Locally grown incense is still for sale in the markets of Hadramaut although the chances are that it is used for food seasoning or as chewing gum, more than for ritual purposes.

The Sabaean/Himyaritic heritage lives on in the collective consciousness of the Yemenis themselves. The distinctive Yemeni identity has its roots in the ancient kingdoms and this was sustained throughout the following Islamic period of history, notably by the contribution of the famous Yemeni scholar and writer al-Hamdani. In a political sense the Sabaean and Himyaritic rule has become a source of inspiration for the future. The desire for reunification often expresses itself by seizing on parallels from the past. History combines with folklore to provide a living framework for the civilisation of Yemen.

The Rise of Islam

Mosque in Djibla. The city was once the capital of Yemen under the legendary Queen Arwa

The period between the decline of the Sabaean state and the dawning of the Islamic era was a brief interlude in the history of Yemen but it was full of incident as the country was rocked by internal tensions triggered off in the combat between the two rival monotheistic faiths. Judaism and Christianity were upheld by warring factions against an anarchic background of tribal paganism.

The last of the Himyarite kings, Dhu Nawas, had converted to Judaism and set about the persecution of the Christian communities. The infamous massacre at Najran brought retribution from the Abyssinians under Abraha, who proved himself to be a militant Christian. The church he built at Sana'a was apparently more magnificent than the popular pagan shrine at Mecca against which he launched the ill-fated "Elephant March" in 570*, symbolically at about the time of the final collapse of the dam at Marib and of the birth of the Prophet Muhammad.

Before the message of the Prophet provided the lasting religion of the entire Arabian peninsula, Yemen underwent a final paroxysm as the anti-Christian Himyar faction invited the Persians to oust the Abyssinians. Yemen became a Persian satrapy. The chaotic state of affairs prevailing in the country at the time is described by Brian Doe in his book *Southern Arabia*: "The moment was now ripe for change. The economy of the country was precarious, the trade routes were falling into disuse, for the area was by-passed by the direct sea trade. Tribal life and prosperity were completely disrupted, religious aspects were brought into disrepute and the tribes were broken up into

*See historical chart, pages 14 and 15.

43

factions for there had never been national stability, and without political organisation anarchy prevailed. It was a situation that could not continue and the time, in Southern Arabia at least, was ready for a new era and a new religious and temporal leader."

Islam was to fill the vacuum which followed the disintegration of the old kingdoms. The ground had been partly prepared by the apparent military superiority of the forces of monotheism over those of the pagan tribes. Conversion was spontaneous and occurred during the lifetime of the Prophet. Mosques were immediately constructed in Sana'a and Janad near Taiz. Badhan, the last of the Persian satraps, embraced Islam, thereby ensuring himself of a governorship. Muhammad sent a number of his companions, including his cousin and son-in-law Ali ibn Abi Talib, to teach the new principles of Islam in Yemen. All the 14,000 members of the powerful Hamdan tribe are said to have embraced Islam in a single day. The Prophet is reported to have been well pleased with his Yemeni converts: "People have come to you from Yemen. They are the most amiable and gentlehearted of men. Faith is of Yemen, and wisdom is Yemeni."

Islam breathed new life into Yemen and at the same time provided the Yemenis with an outlet for their talent and energies. Then as now Yemen was the most populous corner of the Arabian peninsula, and accordingly the armies of Islam which were to sweep all before them drew heavily on Yemeni manpower both for troops and able commanders. Although the internal politics of Yemen continued to follow their particularistic pattern the shaping forces emanated successively from Damascus, Baghdad and Cairo.

The initial impact of Islam was to introduce a sense of cultural unity. Central to the message of Islam is the notion of universality, for the word of Allah as revealed in the Qur'an ordains not just religion but every aspect of social, economic and political life. Submission to the word of Allah therefore implies the adopting of a complete way of life which aims to unite mankind in a universal Muslim brotherhood. Individual salvation and the common social good are the joint benefits of the Islamic faith. The simplicity of the central idea was perhaps its main attraction to a society riddled by the myriad factions of tribal deities.

However, the Islamic world was soon to divide over the vital question of legitimate succession to the authority of the Prophet. One faction saw the role of the Caliph (literally "successor") as a temporal leader to administer Quranic law and provide for defence. According to this view the Caliph was chosen or elected by the ruling establishment. This interpretation was favoured by the Sunni faction against the view of the Shi'a that divine leadership was guaranteed in the descendants of the Prophet through the union of Ali and Fatima, the daughter of the Prophet. Disagreements on genealogy and hence to rights of succession subsequently led to the fragmentation of Shi'a Islam into several minority factions. In Yemen the Zaidi and the Ismaili (or Fatimid) versions of Shi'a were the main contenders for power against the Sunni Umayyad and Abbasid caliphs. The Shi'a-Sunni conflict became immediately problematic in the second half of the 7th century when the rival caliphs Ali and Muawiya both appointed governors to Yemen. This religious and administrative division incidentally provided a handy vehicle to the tribes for the continuation of their traditional factionalism.

The historians divide the period into the Umayyad and Abbasid eras when Yemen was a unit in the Islamic Caliphate and then document a number of contemporaneous or successive dynasties such as the Ziyadids, Ya'furids, Sulayhids, Rasulids, Tahirids and the Imamate. Some of these dynasties aspired to control most of Yemen, but in general two or three distinct kingdoms were establishing themselves in different parts of the country, and these in turn depended on the variable mood of tribal allegiances for their own local power base. As during the time of the ancient kingdoms of Saba and Himyar, there were no clear-cut borders between the states. Each could expand within the territory of Yemen as far as its strength could maintain it. The expansion of one unit meant the contraction of another. This continual vying for power and the resulting upheaval provide the scenario for the thousand years of Yemeni history which followed the coming of Islam.

On the wider political stage the battle for the Caliphate was decided in favour of the Sunni party and a period of Umayyad rule ensued. From 661-749 the Umayyads from their power base in Damascus exercised control over Yemen's destiny. The Umayyad governors with one or two notable exceptions took little interest in Yemeni affairs beyond the extraction of the maximum revenue from taxes imposed on the agricultural peasantry.

This also set the pattern for the Abbasid rule from Baghdad which commenced in 749. The Abbasid governors soon acquired a reputation for oppression and capriciousness in addition to rapacity and indifference. Although Abbasid rule continued in Baghdad until 1258 it was effectively ended in Yemen in 822 when the Banu Ziyad state was set up in Zabid. This marked the first local autonomy movement in Yemen to assert independence against the central authority of the Caliphate. Similar movements sprang up elsewhere, each under the leadership of a war-lord flying one or other banner of the fragmented Islamic community.

Out of the turmoil of "war-lordism" four distinct power centres emerged by the beginning of the 10th century. In addition to the Ziyadi state in Zabid, the Ya'furids of Himyaritic descent established a stronghold in the central highlands and paid only token allegiance to the Abbasid caliph. Meanwhile the Fatimids were successfully planning in the areas of Shi'a persuasion to lay the foundations of their future state. The Fatimid movement, operating through an international underground organisation, aimed to establish a separate state and looked to those provinces of the Islamic empire where the conditions offered the most promise. In 880 two capable representatives were sent to prepare the ground in Yemen. Ali bin al Fadl and Mansur al Yaman conducted a highly sophisticated recruitment campaign. Ali bin al Fadl, following the example of others sent to Yemen, eventually set up his own state in defiance of his Fatimid masters. This first attempt to create a Fatimid Yemen proved premature and the struggle between the Fatimids, the Zaidis and the Ziyadis continued to fester for more than a century without reaching a conclusion.

The Fatimids began their second campaign in the middle of the 11th century. Ali al Sulayhi, Fatimid representative for Yemen, took up the challenge in 1046 and went to war against the Zaidi Imam whom he killed in battle in 1052. This marked the lowest point in the fortunes of the Zaidi Imamate. Apart from a brief interlude during the years 1060 to 1066 no candidate aspired to the Imamate until 1137. The Fatimids in the guise of the Sulayhids held within a substantial degree of unity the territory of the pre-Islamic Himyarite state.

This Yemeni state was characterised by tolerance and good administration. Its authority extended to Hijaz. The Sulayhids are chiefly remembered today for giving Yemen the second of its legendary female characters. Queen as-Sayydah bint Ahmad (famous as Arwa) is cast from the same mould as Bilqis, Queen of Sheba. Yet her credentials are better documented than those of her Sabaean ancestor.

Queen Arwa was entrusted with power when her husband al Mukarram was struck with paraplegia, but she did not really emerge as the power in the land until another competent woman, her mother-in-law Asma, died in 1074. Then for over half a century until 1137, when she died at the age of ninety-two, Queen Arwa exercised effective control over the Fatimid kingdom. Although educated to the same standard as the men of the time, Arwa was clearly aware of the limitations of the female in the realm of tribal politics, and agreed reluctantly to marry in order to comply with the spirit of the age.

Queen Arwa was responsible for a number of important initiatives including the transfer of the capital from Sana'a to Djibla. With her instinctive distrust of unruly manners she persuaded al Mukarram to distance himself from the northern tribes, who were armed to the teeth and to take up residence in the comparative calm and pastoral environment of the mountain valleys to the south. She appears to have devoted her energies to improvements in the local economy, in particular agricultural reform and road building to connect the small villages to regional markets. These roads or tracks can still be identified around Djibla today and the central mosque of the town bears her name.

Doorkeeper at the Great Mosque in Zabid

Unlike the Fatimids with their painstaking efforts to achieve power, the Zaidis had power entrusted to them. The first Imam, Yahya bin Husain bin Qasim al Rassi, was living at Medina when two of the principal clans of Sa'da invited him to come to Yemen as mediator in their tribal disputes. This intimate relationship between the Imamate and the tribes of the north was to be the theme of subsequent Yemeni history. The relationship was never resolved in terms of a durable understanding. The Imams proved unable, even over a thousand years, to achieve an identity of vision with the tribes on whom they remained dependent until the end.

In practical terms Zaidism meant the application of the *sharia*, or Quranic law, and the imposition of the *zakat,* a tax to be devoted to the benefit of common charity. In both respects there was a conflict with customary tribal practice. The Imam was accepted as a mediator of disputes but not always as a law maker and administrator in his own right.

As a political force the Imamate was rather limited in the early years, extending no further south than Sana'a. During the period of the Sulayhid ascendancy it was eclipsed for almost a century and was to survive on the fringe of the Ayyubids and Rasulids who dominated Yemen from the 12th to the 15th centuries. Yet gradually Zaidism established itself in the towns and villages in the north. In the meantime the power and the glory belonged to the Ayyubids and the Rasulids, and the golden age of Islamic Yemen flowered in the south.

The Ayyubid occupation of Yemen from 1173-1229 was accomplished on the orders of the Abbasid caliphs who were anxious to restore allegiance. The task fell to Saladin who dispatched his brother Turanshah to impose the authority of the Baghdad Caliphate. He and two other brothers briefly held

Yemen prior to the accession of the Rasulids.

The family which later established the Rasulid dynasty in Yemen was in the diplomatic service of the Ayyubid court and five Rasulids figured in the Ayyubid conquest of Yemen. The Rasulids came into their own in 1229 and their two centuries of rule coincided with a peaceful and prosperous time in Yemen. The age of imperialism was in abeyance. The colonial powers of Europe had not yet emerged from the chrysalis of the Middle Ages to dominate international trade routes. Yemen was free to pursue her own destiny.

The Rasulids were zealous and efficient tax gatherers but much of the wealth found its way into the development of the country. Two cities in particular, Taiz and Zabid, experienced a boom as Rasulid revenues were channelled into magnificent building projects.

Little is known of Taiz prior to the Rasulid period. The city was chosen as capital by Turanshah on account of its healthy climate and water supply. Set against the lower slopes of the imposing Jebel Sabir, Taiz is best viewed from a high vantage point. Three dazzling white mosques stand out against the surrounding backdrop of mountain, houses, and stone walls. The Muzaffar, Mu'tabiyyah and the Ashrafiyah are the landmarks of the Rasulids in modern Taiz. Unfortunately, they are badly in need of restoration work. ICCROM, the specialist conservation branch of UNESCO, has carried out a survey of the Ashrafiyah, an act which underlines the cultural significance of the building.

Zabid, which served as the winter capital of the Rasulids, is also suffering from the passage of time, but there is enough left of the fine old houses in baked brick painted white with limewash to conjure up an image of its former glory as a sort of Islamic

Oxford, or Heidelberg, possessing some 230 schools devoted to the arts and sciences as well as to the study of the Qur'an. Algebra, it is thought, might have originated in Zabid. The atmosphere of the old Quranic schools lingers on, although Zabid is today a shadow of its former self. In its heyday under the Rasulids Zabid was a major centre of learning, famed throughout the Islamic world.

The decline of Taiz and Zabid reflected the changing fortunes of the Rasulids. Robin Bidwell gives this description of the Rasulids enjoying the peak of their power:

"...flamboyant men of great learning and generosity. One used to picnic in the gardens of Zabid with 300 concubines for company; another sent two ship-loads of gifts to the Sultan of Egypt, which, in addition to Chinese jade, porcelains and brocades, included elephants and giraffes dressed in silk. A palace at Thabat near Taiz was decorated with marble and gold, and the eight gates of Zabid were given gilded pinnacles so that they shone like stars. Learning flourished: a survey showed that there were 230 colleges in Zabid alone. Jurists were honoured by having their works carried to the Sultan on the heads of students to the roll of kettle-drums. Agriculture flourished: special officials supervised irrigation and one of the princes even wrote a scientific treatise on the culture of cereals. The Rasulids were respected abroad and exercised great influence in Mecca. Rulers in Abyssinia and India sent gifts and elephants, and a letter written on pure gold came from the King of Ceylon."*

This glittering world was not destined to last long. At the

*The Two Yemens, pp.13-14.

52

beginning of the 15th century disintegration set in and in 1454 the Rasulid dynasty fell apart through its own internal weakness. The overall effect of the rise of Islam in Yemen was to breathe new life into the tired confusion of the post-Sabaean era. It put Yemen on the world stage and gave Yemenis a new civilisation to replace the old. During the first flourishing of Islam there was a shift away from the old centres at Marib, Shabwa, Timna, and Baraqish to Sa'da, Sana'a, Zabid, Taiz and Aden. Islam gave Yemen not just religion but a social culture and an international language. Nonetheless, the influence of Islam did not stop the continuity of the past and the message of the Qur'an did not fully supplant inherited tribal values and traditions. Modern Yemen is thus an organic blend of ancient Sabaean/Himyaritic and more recent Islamic culture.

The Making of Modern Yemen

The traditional architecture of Yemen is still intact. Some of the houses in Sana'a are 500 years old

At the time of the 1962 Revolution, which put an end to a thousand years of the Zaidi Imamate, there was a memorable quip by an observer of events that Yemen found itself rushing headlong into the 15th century. John Marlowe in *Arab Nationalism and British Imperialism* picked up the same theme: "[Yemen]... perhaps the only remaining country in the world, whose ruling house has successfully defied the onset, not only of the 20th but also of the 19th century."

Certainly, the country had been isolated over most of its territory throughout the dynamic years of change which followed the Industrial Revolution in Europe. Furthermore, a combination of tribal traditionalism and theocratic rule had preserved virtually intact most aspects of mediaeval life. Nevertheless, the easy generalisations mask the fact that parts of Yemen, finding themselves on strategic communications routes, had direct and constant experience from the 16th century onwards through trade links and colonial expansion with Europe and the Ottoman Empire. In fact as early as the beginning of the 16th century there was an event which symbolised the gradual emergence of south Arabia into the mainstream of international development.

The date was 1507 and it marked the occupation by the Portuguese of the island of Socotra, from which they imagined they could control the entrance to the Red Sea. The Portuguese commander, one of the most influential and colourful characters of the colonial era, Afonso de Albuquerque, soon realised that Aden was the key to the region and in 1513 he returned with 1,700 troops to establish dominion.

Through lack of defined purpose and local opposition the Portuguese mission in Yemen was a failure. Yet the visit was significant. It set the pattern of the next 450 years of foreign interest in Aden as a staging point to India and the Far East and it drew Yemen – albeit on the fringe – from a long period of seclusion. In retrospect, the Rasulid period 1229-1454 stands out as the last term of effective and enlightened self-government over the entire Yemen territory.

The failed Portuguese expedition attracted the attention of the Circassian Mamelukes in Cairo, who were also vying for access to the Indian trade – incidentally to the exclusion of the Yemenis. They launched an invasion in 1516, fighting at first in league with the Imamate against the Tahirid regime in Sana'a and then against the Imamate. International developments were, however, about to overtake the Circassians and to demonstrate just how dependent Yemen had become on events way beyond her own borders.

Even as the Circassians were besieging Imam Sharaf al Din in the redoubtable stone fortress of Thula in 1517, news was received that the Ottomans had claimed the Islamic Caliphate, overrun Egypt and were poised to extend sovereignty over the Arabian peninsula. The challenge of the Circassians dissolved and they withdrew to Zabid which they held for the next twenty-two years. The Ottomans stepped in to fill the vacuum and appointed Sulaiman Pasha al Khadim for operations in Yemen.

A massive onslaught began with huge forces of conscripted Egyptian manpower poured into Yemen to subjugate the territory. The Egyptian accountant-general estimated that of the 80,000 soldiers sent to Yemen on behalf of the Ottomans during the years 1526-1547 only 7,000 survived. In 1543 an agreement was reached whereby the Imamate accepted the principle of Ottoman sovereignty while direct control of the territory remained with the Imam. However, this turned out to be no more than a truce in the persisting struggle. In 1565 a general revolt flared up again and threatened to drive the Turks into the Red Sea.

Once more the Governor of Egypt, Sinan Pasha, was obliged to fight back with Egyptian conscripts, and in 1569 he took Taiz, Aden and Sana'a. The Imam Mutahhar maintained a last stronghold in Thula but eventually accepted a truce in 1570. By 1585 the fortunes of the Sharaf al Din princes were at their lowest ebb. They were prisoners of the Ottoman governor who sent them off to Constantinople.

Yemeni nationalism remained dormant until 1598 when Qasim bin Muhammad proclaimed himself Imam with the title of *Mansur Billah* – "Victorious by God". This time Yemeni resistance was strong enough to conduct a successful campaign against the Turks, who were finally expelled in 1636.

In victory the Imamate withdrew into its mediaeval seclusion. Contact with the outside world became limited to the occasional passage of trading ships. International dealings were restricted almost exclusively to the port of Mokha, which, in the second half of the 16th century, had replaced Aden as the principal port of Yemen. The reason was the newly established coffee trade.

The Dutch East India Company took home its first cargo of coffee in 1628. Despite enormous difficulties an international community of Dutch, French and English merchants established itself in Mokha. The boom years of the coffee trade came between 1720-1740. The prosperity of that time can still be seen in the fine old houses, now sadly decaying, which mark the centre of the old town.

Yemen enjoyed a period of external tranquillity in the 18th century but distant events were again to shape its destiny.

Mokha was the port of the Yemen's coffee trade in the 17th-18th centuries.
The remains of the old houses of the merchants can still be seen

Napoleon Bonaparte's invasion of Egypt in 1799 caused the British to fear for the Red Sea trade and communications with India. Consequently the British reappeared off Aden in 1800. The French expedition was short-lived but the Egyptian Viceroy of the Ottoman Sultan proved a more serious threat. Mohammed Ali, having driven the Wahhabi fanatics from the Hijaz, pursued them into the Tihama and extended Egyptian control along the east coast of the Red Sea. This impressed on the British the need to set up their own base to protect and supply their shipping. In 1839 Captain Haines took Aden by force and established the first and only colony of the United Kingdom in Arabia. Only ten years later the Turks returned to Yemen and occupied the Red Sea port of Hodeidah. From this bridgehead they subsequently sought to penetrate the interior. It is from this time that colonial interests and foreign intervention began to draw slowly the lines which were to create two Yemens.

The British authorities in India, only interested in Aden as a coal depot, intended to pursue a strict policy of non-involvement. The reality on the ground was somewhat different. Haines and his successors found themselves constantly drawn into local matters. Still, the British did keep out of the hinterland to a surprising extent and Aden developed as an enclave of modern trade and communications in one of the least explored parts of the world. The opening of the Suez Canal in 1869 brought a dramatic boost to the prosperity and importance of Aden which emerged as a key relay in the network of the expanding British Empire. Within the local context of the southern part of Yemen the colony served as a magnet and a gateway to the world at large.

In the northern part of the country the years 1849-69 were

marked by turmoil and upheaval. There had been a revolt against the Imam who had tried to make a truce with the advancing Turks. The tribes had risen in revolt, driven off the Turks and imprisoned the Imam, who retired to a secluded life in the mountains of Shaharah.

In 1872 the Turks returned to Sana'a. This marked the beginning of a precarious Turkish-Yemeni condominium. Having established a base in Sana'a and wisely ignoring the tribes in the north, the Turks turned their attention to the south of the country and extended their control to Taiz. From this vantage point they loomed large as a threat to the British in Aden. The subsequent rivalry between the two super-powers of the day was to have a lasting effect on the shape of events in Yemen.

The British responded to the Turkish presence by creating a buffer of protectorate states around Aden. A historic process was set in motion. A series of "Treaties of Friendship and Protection" were concluded with the local rulers. This, combined with heavy diplomatic pressure, caused the Turks to back off, but tension continued until the Anglo-Turkish Joint Commission to settle the border dispute between the two super-powers was convened in 1902 at Dhala. The work of the Commission extended over several years before ratification by the two governments involved. In this first formalisation of a political frontier in Yemen the Yemenis themselves were merely spectators.

The Turks, however, were already experiencing the full force of Yemeni nationalism. Ottoman rule had been met with violence from the outset but local resistance remained fragmented until the Imamate was claimed by Muhammad ibn Yahya Hamid al Din. In the 1890s a liberation movement was launched from the traditional Zaidi stronghold of Sa'da in the north. The Imam's declaration stands as a forceful expression of true Yemeni Islamic feeling: "Officials were not giving Allah his due, nor respecting his laws nor those of the prophets of Allah, but they have rather set up unto themselves a religion that was offensive to the sight of Allah and antagonistic to his laws, committing every kind of transgression and leading to the participation therein of those of our people who came into contact with them."

This statement of religious doctrine and Yemeni nationalist sentiment was reiterated with even more vigour by the next Imam who assumed power in 1904. Yahya was perhaps the most potent symbol of Yemeni nationalism. He emerged immediately as a freedom fighter with a call for national revolt against the Turks and laid siege to Sana'a. The Turks were able to fight back but the second siege of Sana'a in 1911 forced them to sign the Treaty of Da'an. This conceded to Imam Yahya control over the highlands as far south as Taiz but allowed the Turks to continue to administer the Tihama.

It is curious that Yahya did not press home his advantage over the Turks and expel them completely, but the Turks proved useful as teachers and advisers and the limited modernisation in Yemen which occurred at the beginning of the century is to the credit of the declining Ottoman rule. Yahya was to remain loyal to the Turks throughout the Great War and he did his utmost to persuade them to remain in Yemen even after their defeat. Although the Turks had officially withdrawn by 1919, several hundred stayed on as private employees of the Imam.

It would appear that with the end of the Turkish occupation Yahya's sense of political purpose faltered. In his later years his image was no longer that of freedom fighter but of mediaeval despot and religious fanatic who sought to regulate every aspect of his subjects' lives. He restricted the modern benefits of education, travel, and technology to a ridiculous degree. "I would rather that my people and I remain poor and eat straw than let foreigners in, or give them concessions, no matter what advantage or wealth might result from their presence." For almost half a century Yemen became a virtual recluse. No foreigners were permitted to enter the country without the express authority of the Imam, nor were Yemenis allowed to travel out.

Nevertheless, the pressures of the modern age proved impossible to resist. The need for training in modern weapons resulted in the sending of Yemeni officer cadets to the Baghdad Military Academy in 1936. This coincided with the officers' successful coup against the Iraqi monarchy, a lesson which was not lost on the cadets nor indeed on Yahya himself who withdrew the Yemenis immediately and arranged henceforth for instructors to come to Yemen. Yet it was too late for such preventive measures. One of the Iraqi instructors, Lt-Col Jamal Jamil, was later among those convicted and executed for their part in the 1948 assassination of Imam Yahya.

In spite of his efforts to shut out change and foreign influence, Yahya did feel himself responsible for the welfare of his people, albeit in a spiritual rather than a material sense. To the outside world he appeared as a reactionary autocrat, holding hostages as a guarantee of good behaviour on the part of the tribes. However, this must be seen against the background of tribal tradition which dominated the conduct of public and private affairs. Even his opponents admitted the deep-rooted sincerity of his purpose but in the long run this was not enough. Adherence to old values could not mask the fact that Yemen was dragging far behind in the economic and social development of the 20th century. Those Yemenis who travelled to foreign countries in defiance of the Imam's ban became immediately aware how backward was their own. The comparison with conditions in Aden was particularly invidious. Within a hundred years of its founding as a British colony, Aden had progressed from a small town to the most prosperous port on the Arabian peninsula. In 1937 Aden became a Crown colony administered from London instead of being ruled through India. Shipping continued to boom; by the mid-1950s only London, Liverpool and New York handled more ships, and a quarter of a million shoppers descended on the Aden *suq* from the port in the course of a year. Thus the two worlds of modernity symbolised by Aden and extreme conservatism represented by Sana'a co-existed in the same country.

There was a large exodus of Yemenis via Aden to the Far East, the United Kingdom and the United States. At the end of the Second World War the Aden colony became a centre for dissenters in exile from the rule of the Imam. "The Free Yemenis" conducted from the British colony a propaganda campaign which aimed to liberalise without abolishing the institution of the Imamate. The defection of one of Yahya's own sons to "The Free Yemenis" demonstrated the wide range of support for the movement. The original plan to await the death of the ageing Imam was abandoned in 1948 in favour of an assassination plot. The bloody deed was duly carried out, but the coup failed because of lack of experience to act properly, and the failure to gain enough sympathy either with the Yemenis or the neighbouring Arab countries. The plotters were rapidly out-manoeuvred by Yahya's son Ahmad, who reasserted the rule of the Mutawakkilite Kingdom. He rewarded the tribes for their support by giving over the city of Sana'a for three days of sacking and pillage.

Ahmad conducted affairs throughout his reign from the southern city of Taiz until his death in 1962. Ahmad, in contrast to his father, did display in his youth some sympathy with liberal ideas and he opened the door for international involvement in Yemen's development. Nevertheless, his readiness to embrace the modern age was severely limited. Like Yahya he thought he could turn back the clock. After the overthrow of King Farouk of Egypt in 1952, Ahmad ordered the confiscation of all radio sets in public places in an effort to shut out the dangerous influence of political revolution. Within a week of Imam Ahmad's death there followed the 1962 Revolution which demanded not only the removal of the Imam but the abolition of the Imamate itself. This laid the foundation of the contemporary state of the Yemen Arab Republic and signified a new chapter in the progress of Yemeni civilisation.

But the immediate aftermath of the Revolution was the Civil War which lasted until 1968. In this conflict Yemen became the battleground for the Royalists, backed by Saudi money, against the Republicans, who were supported by Egyptian troops. The closing stage of the Civil War was fought out between the Yemenis themselves. The failure of the Royalists to overcome the heroic seventy days' resistance (1 December, 1967 to February, 1968) of the Republicans during the crucial siege of Sana'a eventually decided the outcome. Ahmad's son al Badr was forced to concede the futility of his cause. He retired to England as the last reigning representative of the thousand year-old Imamate.

The traditional power structure in the southern part of Yemen adminstered by Britain was to undergo a more cataclysmic change. Aden had developed in its own cosmopolitan fashion. Population statistics from 1955 reveal the following breakdown of ethnic groups: of a total of 138,000 there were only 37,000 Aden Yemenis, but 48,000 immigrant Yemenis, 19,000 from the Protectorates, 15,000 Indians, 10,000 Somalis, 5,000 Europeans (nearly all from Britain) and 1,000 Jews. By contrast, the hinterland consisted of a tribal society basically unchanged in its essential structure since the introduction of Islam, or even before.

Seen in retrospect, the British attempt to create a Federation from the tribal society of southern Arabia was a doomed enterprise. In any case, the attempt to set up a new state fell victim to the politics of expediency as the United Kingdom tried to extricate itself with unseemly haste from imperial commitments. Under the mounting pressure of the liberation movement the British withdrew in 1967. The southern part of Yemen, known at first as the People's Republic of South Yemen, emerged after the "Corrective Step of 1969" as the People's Democratic Republic of Yemen. This coincided with the declaration of the constitution of the Yemen Arab Republic in the north in 1970.

Today the governments of both states are committed to the principle of reunification within the framework of the common cultural heritage which extends back at least three thousand years.

The sense of unity is real and deep, but the exact nature of its political expression is yet to be resolved. Modern Yemen is still in the making.

Sana'a, capital of the Yemen Arab Republic, traces its origins back to Sabaean times. Yet its development is entirely of the Islamic period. The old city is still intact although modern buildings now stand on the outskirts

The distinctive architecture of Sana'a results from the subtle combination of simple materials. The lower storeys of stone support the upper floors of baked brick decorated with limewash. Each house is a single family residence

Islam reached Yemen within the lifetime of the Prophet. The city of Sana'a contains many traditional mosques. The minarets use the same materials as the houses but with their contrasting forms create a varied skyline

The Great Mosque in Sana'a is built on Sabaean foundations as can be seen from the angular shape of some of the columns. Reading from the Qur'an is part of the daily devotions of practising Muslims

Street scenes in Sana'a present a revealing picture of local life. Much of the shopping is still done by the men. Women wear austere black dresses or cover themselves with brightly coloured cloth when walking in the city

The mafraj *occupies pride of place in the Yemeni house. This room is usually located on the top storey and affords panoramic views. Light enters through the stained glass fanlights to create colourful patterns*

The "Palace on the Rock" at Wadi Dahr near Sana'a is the best known of the numerous Imam's palaces scattered over the country. Some of these former royal residences have now been converted for use as hotels

Sa'da, the northernmost city in Yemen, is composed entirely of mud. The distinctive shape of the buildings comes from the construction technique of superimposing layers of mud, lifted at the corners for better stability

Sa'da's wall is still intact. The use of mud creates an effect of homogeneity, both in colour and texture, between the city and the ground on which it stands. Some of the houses are, however, gaily decorated

Baked brick makes an occasional appearance in Sa'da and creates a striking effect against the overall background of mud. The city has been described as halfway between sculpture and architecture

Wadi Hadramaut

Shibam, the main city of this unique valley civilisation in the south of the country, is an assemblage of mud skyscrapers extending up to nine storeys in height. Some of the houses are five hundred years old

In contrast to the highly urbanised environment of the closely packed houses, the
streets of Shibam present aspects of country life. Goats, chickens, donkeys and even
camels roam through the alleyways and open squares

The technique of mud-brick making can still be observed. The basic ingredients of earth, water and straw are moulded into bricks using a wooden frame. Once dried in the sun, the bricks are stacked for use. More mud serves as cement

Some amazing constructions are possible with mud-brick which completely mask the original material. One spectacular example is the mosque at Terim. Mud is still used in Hadramaut for a modern building such as an airport or hotel

The Sultan's Palace at Seyun is another mud-brick construction which has been boldly disguised by the use of a fanciful limewash decoration. The wedding-cake effect is a characteristic feature of Hadramaut architecture

The town of Seyun offers the calm seclusion of hand-crafted mosques which attain a harmonious simplicity. Popular festivals, such as the day of the Prophet Hud, are occasions for colourful costumes and dancing in the street

Mountain Strongholds

Hajjara is the most formidable of Yemen's mountain strongholds. The houses are grouped together to provide their own defensive rampart against any intruders. The mountain itself defines the shape and limits of the village

The houses of Hajjara are constructed without mortar. The blocks of stone are cut to fit and smaller pieces of stone are inserted to secure the structure. Different colours of stone can be used to good effect

The mountain terraces of Yemen help to conserve water and prevent soil erosion. They are the dominant feature of the landscape and extend almost to the summits of the mountains, using every available scrap of land

The origins of the terraces are lost in antiquity, but it is likely that they date back to the end of the Sabaean era in the 6th century and came into their own after the final collapse of the dam at Marib

Thula, a small fortified town within easy reach of Sana'a, demonstrates the harmony of stone employed in a variety of functions

The roads and houses, being of the same stone, create a strong sense of organic unity. The town is literally a part of the mountainside

The town of Huth appears in the distance as a continuation of the landscape

The rocky terrain is relieved by unexpected expanses of fertile green

Mukalla, the main port of the Hadramaut, is still a living example of traditional ways and trading activities. It is a vital link between the desert hinterland and maritime commerce

Characteristic sights along the coast: A fishing boat returns to Bir Ali (top).
Fresh limes offered for sale in the market at Mukalla (bottom)

Aden owes its strategic importance to the volcanic terrain which provides the best natural setting on the Arabian Peninsula for such vast port facilities. Aden's trading links with India and China go back more than 2000 years

The town itself is not distinguished by Arabian architecture. The familiar forms of modern international buildings and street patterns are the main feature of Aden, in marked contrast to the towns of the interior

Southern Highlands

Taiz is the main city of the region. Little is known of its origins prior to the Rasulid period (1229-1454) except that Saladin's brother favoured the site for its healthy climate and water supply

*The remains of the Rasulid period are today the major Islamic monuments of Taiz.
Just outside the city is the mosque of Al Janad (bottom right) which was founded
during the lifetime of the Prophet*

Djibla, once the capital of the legendary Queen Arwa, is today a significant market town

The narrow streets of Djibla provide for human encounters at every turn

Tihama

Hodeidah is the main fishing port of Yemen's Red Sea coastal plain, the Tihama.
The fish market is held right next to the beach

Hodeidah, although it now has modern commercial facilities, still retains the traditional style of the street markets

Bait al Faqih is the market place of the Tihama. The suq *is a colourful affair with active female participation*

112

Local products include tobacco, cotton, bananas, papaya, straw hats and pottery.
Friday is market day

The qat *market in Bait al Faqih. The* qat *leaves are chewed over in order to extract the mildly narcotic juices*

Most Yemini males chew qat *regularly and its consumption can account for a large portion of family expenditure*

Silk and cotton weaving is a speciality of Bait al Faqih. The weavers work in the open under makeshift sunshades. The brightly coloured lengths of cloth can be purchased in the local suq *as well as in Sana'a*

Typical face of the Tihama. This gentleman is a native of Zabid

Zabid displays an architectural style all its own. Baked bricks are painted with limewash. Sometimes the bricks are arranged to create monochrome decorative patterns

Zabid was once a major centre of Islamic learning. In its prime during the Rasulid period there were some 230 Quranic schools. Nowadays trade is the main activity of the town

The Great Mosque of Zabid still draws young people

Learning to recite from the Qur'an is the object of this classroom session

The Ancient Kingdoms

The site of the ancient port of Qana (top), near present day Bir Ali, was the beginning of one of the incense routes which converged on Shabwa, capital of the Kingdom of Hadramaut (bottom) for the long overland trek north

At Marib there are remains of temples buried in the sand and the enormous sluice-gates (bottom) that stood at either end of the Marib dam which irrigated enough land to support an estimated 300,000 people

125

Sabaean art is distinctly south Arabian in style. This bronze statue of a notable man named Ma'di Karib was found at Marib and has been dated between 500-200 BC. (National Museum, Sana'a)

Votive stela in alabaster with female carved in high relief (top) c 500 BC.
Head of a woman in alabaster (bottom left) AD 100-400. Head of a man in alabaster
(bottom right), 500-100 BC. (National Museum, Sana'a)

The Advance of the Explorers

The rugged mountains of Yemen helped deter all but the most determined of explorers

"Arabia, a land larger than peninsular India, lies in the heart of the Old World, and beside its main road of commerce, but we know much of it hardly better than the Antarctic continent." So begins D. G. Hogarth's classic work *The Penetration of Arabia* published in 1904. Arabia has since been inexorably opened up and exposed to the scrutiny of the West. As social change and the rush to the new cities of the oil age has destroyed much of traditional life, so has the urge to explore diminished in equal proportion. Yet the age of exploration is not over, especially in Yemen, that part of Arabia which has for long been a challenge to travellers.

The British journalist David Holden described in *Farewell to Arabia* the mystique still surrounding Yemen in the Fifties: "Secluded behind its mountain barriers, protected by its sheer lack of physical communications and the fitful hostility of its Imams, the Yemen maintained a reputation of unusual mystery, even for Arabia. . . . a medieval survival, a kingdom of silence." A visitor to Sana'a in the 1980s would find the silence rudely shattered by the din of progress, but the essential truth of the statement remains.

It is difficult to define exactly what distinguishes an explorer from an ordinary traveller. Hogarth (*op cit*) wrote: "Almost all Arabian explorers may be said to have been impelled to the peninsula by their own curiosity or that of foreign princes and associations . . ." Yet in the case of Yemen the promise of commercial gain often came before that of scientific interest.

The ill-fated expedition of Aelius Gallus in 24 BC sent by Augustus in order to bring within the Roman orbit that country of Arabia Felix renowned for its frankincense, myrrh and other luxuries, may be taken as the beginning of both exploration and of foreign interest in Yemen. Aelius Gallus, the Eparch of

Egypt, suffered great hardship and brought home none of the anticipated riches. His army of 25,000 was virtually annihilated, having penetrated from the Hijaz as far as Marib, although there is a possibility that he actually reached Shabwa. The Romans, later to be emulated by the Turks, used Egyptian manpower for their military incursion into Yemen.

Thereafter for several centuries newcomers to Yemen were sailors and merchants. The anonymous Greek sea captain and author of the *Periplus of the Erythraean Sea* (c AD 150) described the land as perceived from the sea as well as from information gathered at the ports. Marco Polo called at Aden around 1220 and the famous Arab traveller Ibn Battutah visited Yemen after his stay in Mecca in 1328. In 1487 Pero de Couilha, commissioned by the King of Portugal, skirted the coasts of Arabia, calling three times at Aden. The first European to penetrate the interior was almost certainly the Italian adventurer Ludovico di Varthema in 1503.

Varthema's account was published in Italian at Rome in 1510. His main motivation was "to follow out a desire after novel things" and this led him into several dangerous situations. Arrested as a spy and taken from Aden to Sana'a, whence he escaped by feigning madness, Varthema found his way back to Aden and freedom. Hogarth does not, however, give him full marks as an explorer: "His is a scant record. More account, for example, might have been expected of the great buildings in Sana'a. But so far as it went, it proved that the ancient fertility of Yemen was no myth, and that a relatively high civilisation was still flourishing in the spice lands." Varthema's account remained the only available source of European information on Yemen for almost two hundred years.

The great Portuguese colonialist Afonso de Albuquerque appeared at Aden in 1513 en route to Goa but his attempt to take the port was thwarted. The great man then followed his imperial destiny on to India, leaving barely a trace of his passing in Yemen. Two Iberian Jesuits, also in the service of the Portuguese in India, found themselves marooned in 1590 in Hormuz and were taken as prisoners through the Wadi Hadramaut to Sana'a.* The two Jesuits, after five years detention in Sana'a, were permitted to continue their journey to Abyssinia.

At the beginning of the 17th century the coffee trade in Mokha introduced a new breed of visitor to Yemen. In 1609 the British merchant John Jourdain was the first of many merchants to make the trek up from the Red Sea coast to the mountain city of Sana'a in order to seek permission to set up in trade. His application was refused. His successor in 1610, Sir Henry Middleton fared worse. Taken to Sana'a where he spent two months in prison with "grief of heart and a multitude of rats", as sole companions, Sir Henry was eventually returned to Mokha whence he escaped in a barrel. Perhaps due to the circumstances of his stay Sir Henry Middleton did not leave much account of Yemen. He remembered Sana'a as a city "somewhat larger than Bristol, well built of stone and lime."

In spite of the local difficulties, the Dutch and the British had established themselves in Mokha by the 1620s. After the expulsion of the Turks from Yemen in 1636 the treatment of

*This entry into Yemen "through the back door" was not to be repeated by another European until the daring journey of the German photographer, Hans Helfritz in 1934.

foreigners improved somewhat. French merchants also came to trade in coffee. In 1710 two Frenchmen from St Malo, the surgeon Barbier and Major de la Grelaudière, were summoned to attend the ailing eighty-seven year-old Imam. An account of their journey, somewhat imprecise, was rendered to Louis XIV.

European interest in Yemen was soon aroused to the point where the chance accounts of unqualified observers were no longer sufficient to satisfy scientific curiosity. A turning point in the exploration of Yemen came with the Danish expedition largely accredited to Carsten Niebuhr. In fact Niebuhr was but one of a group of five specialists on the mission sponsored by the Danish King Frederick V, which travelled in Yemen during 1762-64. In addition to Niebuhr, a German surveyor and map-maker, the party consisted of Professor Friedrich von Haven, philologist; Georg Baurenfeind, artist and engraver; Christian Kramer, doctor; Peter Forsskal, scientist and botanist. Berggren, the Swedish manservant to the group, was the sixth member. They were instructed to act as equals with no one in the role of expedition leader and each was to pursue his own line of enquiry as well as to assist the others. The strains and tensions of the trip were perhaps inevitable but the physical toll was indeed terrible.

Carsten Niebuhr was the sole survivor of the expedition to return home and his account, soberly entitled *Description of Arabia*, was in effect a masterly synthesis of the work and observations of the entire group. Niebuhr found high academic acclaim for his terse, objective style, never intruding with his own feelings. The consistent understatement, so rare in travel accounts, renders even more poignant the tragic destiny which befell first Professor von Haven, who died of malaria on 24th May 1763, and then Forsskal on 10th July of the same year.

Traditional Tihama transport

Niebuhr's description of Forsskal's demise under miserable conditions in Terim demonstrates the style of the narrative: "We were deeply affected at his loss. In consequence of his botanical excursions he has learned more than any of us of the Arabic tongue, and its different dialects. Fatigue, or the want of conveniences, never discouraged him; he could accommodate himself to the manners of the people of the country, without doing which, indeed, no one can hope to travel with advantage through Arabia." Baurenfeind and Berggren died on the onward voyage to India where Kramer also succumbed to the fever.

Despite the obvious discomforts and danger, Niebuhr recorded: "... we found the inhabitants of Yemen in such a state of civilisation, that we could travel among them with the same safety as in Europe." He noted that the Arabs and that Yemen called for no exceptional courage, and neither promised nor afforded exciting or romantic adventure.

The party was received hospitably by the Imam, whose return from the mosque on Friday left a lasting impression on the visitors: "Beside the princes of the blood, there were in this procession at least six hundred noblemen, ecclesiastics and officers, civil and military, all superbly mounted upon horses; and a vast crowd of people followed on foot. On each side of the Imam was borne a standard, having upon it a small silver box filled with amulets, whose efficacy was imagined to render him invincible. This procession was, in short, magnificent, but disorderly. The riders paced or galloped, at pleasure, and all went on in confusion."

Niebuhr did not visit Marib but offered his own view of the decline of Sabaean power: "The tradition that the city of Marib was destroyed by a deluge, occasioned by the sudden bursting of the wall, has entirely the air of a popular fable. It seems more probable that the wall, being neglected, fell gradually into disrepair, when the kingdom of the Sabaeans declined."

Of the political structure of Yemen in the 18th century Niebuhr writes: "... the state of Yemen is not unlike to that of Germany. The Arabs want only a head; they have princes, a body of nobility, and an aristocratic league. But their constitution is not of recent origin; nor did it take its rise in the forests. It is as ancient as society itself, and will probably last while the country endures in which nature has established it." Niebuhr's account did not achieve popularity outside academic circles and the unassuming pioneer of scientific exploration was not to travel again after his epic journey. Niebuhr was also the last great traveller of the 18th century to visit Yemen. The 19th century was to send forth people of widely differing calibre and motivation.

The next generation of explorers was a mixed crew. There were men with missionary zeal such as Joseph Wolff, the son of a German rabbi, who felt called to convert oriental Jews to the Anglican faith which he had himself espoused. Wolff's visit to Sana'a in 1836 was not a success, partly on account of his lack of Arabic. From the same mould and with the same mission was the Reverend Henry Aaron Stern, whose journey to Sana'a twenty years later left both the Jewish and the Muslim populations unimpressed.

The visits of two naturalists at the beginning of the 19th century stand as symbols of the growing specialisation in scientific enquiry. Ulrich Jasper Seetzen, botanist and orientalist, apparently in the Russian service, entered Yemen about 1810 from the Hijaz. He was murdered in circumstances which remain shrouded in mystery. Paul Emile Botta, the French botanist and physician to the Egyptian Viceroy Mohammed Ali, was commissioned by the Museum of Natural History at Paris to collect samples of flora in Yemen. His journey in 1836 took him to the highlands of southern Yemen and he achieved the first ascent of Mount Sabir behind Taiz.

Meanwhile in the south, Wellsted and Cruttenden from the British naval survey ship *Palinurus* had made the first forays into the great hinterland from the ports of Aden and Mukalla. The inscriptions which they brought back from their voyage in 1834/5 furnished the first conclusive evidence that Himyaritic records from the ancient kingdoms of south Arabia still survived. Niebuhr had only heard reports of the existence of such. This discovery triggered off a series of expeditions conducted by archaeologists or at least inspired by curiosity concerning the pre-Islamic civilisations of Saba and Himyar.

These new explorers were, however, preceded by one of the great Arabian adventurers, Adolf von Wrede, a Bavarian soldier of fortune, who reached Wadi Doan from Mukalla in 1843. He travelled disguised as a pilgrim but it must have worn thin, for at the town of Sif he was attacked by a mob and hauled before the local shaikh as a spy. He was lucky to be released with the loss of his notes and baggage. Captain Haines in Aden received a brief report from von Wrede and passed it on in 1844 to the Royal Geographical Society in London. Von Wrede was not taken seriously until 1870 when his account *Reise in Hadramut* was eventually published in Germany. Possibly his scientific descriptions were too graphic and lacked the method of precise observation favoured at the time.

Proper exploration of Wadi Hadramaut did not take place until the end of the 19th century. The British in Aden did not encourage as a matter of policy too much involvement with the tribes of the hinterland. Hogarth points out in *Penetration of Arabia*: "There was much truth in the complaint made in 1889 by the German botanist and explorer, Schweinfurth, that the British authorities in Aden had done almost nothing in 50 years to dispel the darkness which brooded over southern Arabia." In the 1930s Harry St John Philby was to complain more vociferously of the obstructive attitude of the British.

Perhaps on account of this, the most significant journeys of exploration to Yemen in the middle of the 19th century were to the northern part of the country. Marib and the legend of the Queen of Sheba attracted mainly the French and Germans to Yemen's desert fringe. Louis Arnaud was the first to reach Marib in 1843; "a most remarkable exploration"*, during which Arnaud although plagued by ill-health and harassed by the tribes succeeded in bringing back about fifty Himyaritic transcriptions.

Joseph Halévy was the next on the trail in 1869. Under the aegis of the "Académie des Inscriptions" of Paris, Halévy managed to visit Ma'in, Marib, and Nagran. He brought back a total of 685 inscriptions, which represented more than a tenfold increase in knowledge of pre-Islamic Arabia at that time.

Between 1877 and 1880 the Italian, Alessandro Manzoni, made three visits to Sana'a, but without adding significantly to current knowledge of Yemen. However, his sketches of Sana'a were the first visual impression of the unique architecture of the city and remained the most accurate record until the advent of the photographer-explorers at the turn of the century.

In 1882 the Austrian scholar Eduard Glaser commenced his explorations of the central plateau. In four visits to Yemen between 1882 and 1894 he succeeded in obtaining about two

*Hogarth, *op cit.*

137

thousand copies of the epigraphical evidence of the old kingdoms. With strong protection from the Turkish military, Glaser was able to spend thirty days at Marib and he copied nearly four hundred Himyaritic inscriptions as well as drawing a sketch survey of the site. Glaser's contribution is an important landmark in the history of South Arabian studies.

Sana'a received the visit of one last adventurer in the 19th century. Walter Harris bluffed his way from Aden in 1892 and after a brief spell in prison made his way to the sea via Manakha: "Wonderful, stupendous it was! Around us on all sides the bare fantastic peaks and perpendicular precipices, on the edge of one of which we perched... of all the places that it has ever been my lot to see, Manakha is the most wonderfully situated." The enthusiastic Englishman was to be the last explorer in the north for some time. The liberation campaign against the Turkish occupation which followed the accession of Imam Yahya in 1904 made the country extremely perilous. Only one other British adventurer, Arthur Wavell, found his way – at great personal risk – to Sana'a and Marib in 1908.

At the end of the 19th century attention was shifting to that last great secret of Arabia, Wadi Hadramaut. This vast inland valley, locked in a desert plateau, had long followed its own particular pattern of development. Shielded from the surrounding desert by the soaring walls of the wadi and yet with access via the ports of Shihr and Mukalla to East Africa, India and the Orient, the Wadi was at once insular and international. There was at times little intercourse with the rest of Arabia but a steady outflow of manpower from it to more distant places. Over the years poverty had driven out hundreds of thousands of people to seek their fortunes in Java, Singapore, Zanzibar and India. Then through the British colony at Aden the emigration movement extended to the United Kingdom and to America. Yet such was the power of the home valley that the migrants would always return in old age after careers spent on the other side of the world. Indeed, the economy of the valleys depended largely on remittances from the Far East for its daily survival. Niebuhr had noted the following from information given by one of the inhabitants of the Wadi: "What was particularly striking in the lists of names mentioned to me, was the remarkable resemblance of the names of many of the present cities in Hadramaut, to those of cities of Arabia spoken of by the most ancient historians. Many of these establishments must have existed in the same state from the most remote antiquity." It was the twin goals of uncovering traces of the pre-Islamic Kingdom of Hadramaut and the documenting of a society effectively insulated from contemporary development that spurred on yet a new wave of explorers.

The first to penetrate the main Wadi Hadramaut was the German Arabic scholar and archaeologist Leo Hirsch. In 1893 he managed to reach the famed city of mud skyscrapers, Shibam, and despite a cool reception there was able to proceed to Terim. However, he did not discover the "royal ruins" mentioned by von Wrede. As for Hirsch's own travel account, Robin Bidwell in his book *Travellers in Arabia* states "...exactly what one might expect from a deeply learned Teuton." Be that as it may, Leo Hirsch had reopened the exploration of Wadi Hadramaut after an interval of fifty years following von Wrede's attempt.

Later in the same year the remarkable couple Theodore and Mabel Bent followed the same route as Hirsch. Although the information they brought back was less instructive than that of

Hirsch, the Bents did take photographs and produced the first popular book on the Hadramaut. The Bents travelled in an oddly assorted group which included an Indian surveyor, a botanist from Kew, a Greek servant and an Egyptian naturalist. They moved as if in a tiny capsule of foreign attitudes, forever vigilant against contact with the natives. Yet, in spite of the considerable hardships encountered, the Bents were able to appreciate the unique civilisation and architectural beauty of the Hadramaut cities.

After this journey there was an interval of almost forty years during which Wadi Hadramaut was permitted to slumber on undisturbed by the persistence of explorers. Then in the 1930s a new wave of travellers appeared on the scene. Within a space of three years, 1933-36, Van der Meulen, Dutch diplomat; Hermann von Wissmann, German cartographer; Harold Ingrams, British political officer, with his wife Doreen; Hans Helfritz, German photographer; Freya Stark, English travel writer; and Harry St John Philby, English explorer and adviser to the Saudi monarch, all launched forth – some with and some without official backing – to throw themselves on the mercy of the Hadramaut. In the published accounts of these travels one detects an undercurrent of one-upmanship and professional jealousy which sometimes mars the real achievements.

Van der Meulen and von Wissmann set off from Aden in April 1931 and headed via the port of Mukalla towards Wadi Hadramaut. Unlike the experience of previous travellers theirs was, in the words of their publisher C. Snouck Hurgronje, "a triumphal progress". Perhaps times were changing and certainly Van der Meulen's linguistic ability and genuine sympathy for the people proved to be a great asset. The account of their journey *Hadramaut — Some of its Mysteries Unveiled* is full of rewarding personal encounters and anecdotes. Writing of the wily bedouin: "They enjoyed laughing, and if one could manage to maintain one's hold on them by keeping them in good humour, it was possible to crack many a hard nut." Elsewhere it is recorded: "It is perhaps here timely to pay tribute to the wonderful hospitality of the Arabs. Who, in the West, would hide his disappointment at having a wedding feast broken in upon by a whole caravan of tired and hungry men? Who amongst us would immediately throw open his whole house to the travellers, 'the sons of the road', himself bring water to slake their thirst, and immediately prepare food to strengthen them?"

Van der Meulen's real interest as Dutch consul was to establish relations with the Hadramis who had resided in the Dutch colonies of the East Indies. Van der Meulen documents the phenomenon of emigration from Hadramaut: "Everything that is fine and prosperous owes its existence to money that is earned abroad. The tie between a Hadrami and his birth place is very close, and if he is doing well, he returns from time to time, and when he sees the evening of his life approaching he longs to spend it in the little mud town where he was born, and finally, to await the Day of Resurrection in Hadrami soil, which for him is consecrated ground."

One of the best known visitors to Wadi Hadramaut was the lady traveller in Arabia and popular writer, Freya Stark. Her goal was to be the first European to reach Shabwa, the abandoned site of the original capital city of the Kingdom of Hadramaut. On 8th January 1935 she wrote from Aden: "Shabwa is not going to be a small matter as it appears to mean seven long days with no water, and an unknown quantity on the other side owing to the impossibility of knowing where one will go and to the fact that the Imam's people take you straight to prison."

Freya Stark's difficulties were compounded by an illness which laid her low and ultimately prevented her from reaching her goal.

Freya Stark's disappointment must have been rendered less bitter by the testimonial given by her friends in the Hadramaut: "This is a certificate to Miss Freya Stark, English, traveller, that she is conversant with laws and guided by religion, and of an honourable house, and is the first woman to travel from England to Hadramaut alone – and is mistress of endurance and fortitude in travel and the suffering of terrors and danger."

Despite his antics and flair for near disaster Hans Helfritz, the German photographer, succeeded in reaching Shabwa and continued by way of the desert fringe of the Empty Quarter in the company of a bedouin caravan to arrive at Sana'a by entering Yemen "through the back door", the first record of this journey being accomplished by a European since that of the Iberian Jesuits in 1590. Helfritz's account: *Yemen — A Secret Journey* is entertaining and well illustrated even if lacking in scholarship and extravagant in some of its claims. Furthermore, the famous Harry St John Philby gallantly admits that Helfritz beat him to Shabwa by a full eighteen months. In his book *Sheba's Daughters*, concerning his 1936 explorations, Philby took pains to vindicate the reputation of the German: "... while the outraged citizens of Shabwa were discussing over his coffee and breakfast not whether to kill him, but how to kill him, Helfritz slipped out with his two cameras to 'shoot' the ruins. In the midst of this operation he was set upon by the mob, and escaped with his escort through a hail of wild fire, taking snapshots the while as he led the way out of danger. He probably did not have more than an hour of daylight in the place. Yet he made good use of it, and his courage and coolness in the face of a very real danger deserve the warmest recommendation."

Whatever Philby's motives were in promoting Helfritz, the veteran Arabian explorer showed himself to be more circumspect. His investigation of the ruins at Marib was conducted from the safety of a hilltop some half a mile distant from the site. That Philby was probably not shamming danger received adequate confirmation in 1951 when the Wendell Phillips expedition for the "American Foundation for the Study of Man" had to escape from warring tribes at Marib by cool subterfuge and a good dose of luck.

In a sense the age of exploration can now be considered closed. All the major sites have been visited and most are accessible. However, in some areas the degree of security will depend on the circumstances at that time. The tourism authorities have now stepped in to ensure that visitors do not have to run the risks of earlier explorers.

Yet if today the dangers have been minimised, the mystery still lingers. Writing of the Hadramaut in 1937 Freya Stark commented: "... the then scarcely visited smaller valleys of the Hadramaut seemed to be separated by centuries rather than by space from the life of Europe; I thought constantly of some illuminated manuscript, roughly painted with draped, sandalled figures and crowded backgrounds of towns, coming suddenly awake and living and moving beyond its frame; and ... history ... will never again be merely history to me, since I have lived in it and known what it has been." That sense of things past is still present throughout Yemen; so in another sense the age of exploration is perhaps not yet over.

Travel in Yemen

Vehicles of the Yemen Tourism Company at Shabwa, the site of the ancient capital of the Kingdom of Hadramaut

The mystery of the past and the thrill of discovery remain to be experienced afresh. Nevertheless, modern accommodation awaits the traveller in the major centres of Sana'a, Taiz, Aden, Mukalla and Hodeidah as well as in some of the smaller towns such as Sa'da and Hajja. The hotels range from those of the international chains to more modest locally-run establishments. Of particular charm are the traditional Yemeni style *funduqs*, many of them residences of the Imams in the past, which give the visitor a unique chance to sample the feeling of Yemeni architecture from within.

There is one such almost within sight of Sana'a International Airport. The Rawdah Palace Hotel is a tall stone building set among lush vineyards behind mud walls. The rooms, cool and peaceful within the huge masonry, afford distant views of the minarets and lofty houses of Sana'a. Closer to the centre of the city is another Imam's palace, the Dar Al Hamd, which also serves as a hotel. In the top floor room of the traditional Yemeni house, known as the *mafraj*, Yemeni male social activity has its exclusive abode. The *mafraj* with its panoramic views is the crown of the traditional Yemeni house. Its four sides are lined with mattresses and cushions; the middle of the room is left open. The walls are without decoration save perhaps for a pattern worked in the gypsum. Light enters through the windows from all sides and is gently diffused by the soft whiteness of the walls. Dramatic dashes of blue, red, green, and yellow are added through the stained glass pieces of the fanlights set above each window.

The *mafraj* is the best vantage point from which to savour Yemeni life. Not only are the views from the top of the house so much more revealing than those afforded at street level; the *mafraj* is also the nucleus of social life. It is essentially a male preserve used for receiving visitors, relaxing, chatting, eating, and chewing the narcotic leaves of *qat*. It is a fact that most important matters in Yemen are discussed and resolved during lengthy afternoon *qat* sessions, so the *mafraj* functions equally as a council chamber and living room. Here, as with many other aspects of Arab custom, there is a greater unity between public and private affairs than in the West.

In some of the local country hotels the *mafraj* serves additionally as dormitory for passing travellers. At Manakha, perched high in the mountains between Sana'a and Hodeidah, or in the rocky fortress town of Thula a night spent on the mattresses of the *mafraj* is a magic experience, like being an eagle at rest in a lofty eyrie. From the defensive stronghold the view scans vast tracts of country, the sky feels very close and the walls thick and secure.

Stone architecture in Thula

An almost opposite effect can be achieved by going underground, for example into one of the public bath houses of Sana'a. This is a bold undertaking and it is better that the stranger should take along a local Yemeni to explain the procedure and agree the price with the bathkeeper. Here one is centuries removed from today's world of gleaming shower fittings and sanitary refinements. Water is poured by hand in alternate dousings of hot and cold. The rough woollen mitten of the bathkeeper removes not just surface dirt but also several layers of skin. Yet it is worthwhile submitting to the experience. Emerging, freshly scrubbed, from the subterranean gloom of the *hammam*, the visitor feels that he has survived an ancient initiation ritual and become an intimate of the city.

The recurrent sense of intimacy is perhaps one of the most striking features of a visit to Yemen. The people respond to strangers with a fine balance of open friendliness and discrete

Jacket salesman in Sana'a. Traditional retail techniques survive

reserve. Whether wandering through the dusty *suqs* of the cities or the labyrinthine backstreets of the mountain villages there is always an interchange of smiles and greetings. The tiniest knowledge of Arabic is rewarded out of all proportion. The single word *tammam* is the passport to the country. Meaning simply "good" or "fine", it can be used either as a statement or a question or both at the same time and invariably draws forth a smile or a greeting. To visit Yemen just for its scenery and culture is to experience only half of the pleasure. Above all Yemen is its people. Memories of open faces and laughter-filled voices remain long after the views of Imam's palaces, mountain peaks, and Sabaen pillars have faded away.

As a counter-balance to the spontaneous friendliness of public places the privacy of family life and the modesty of the women are tightly maintained. The houses do not have windows on the ground floor and the courtyards are usually protected from view behind huge, heavy doors. The mosques may be visited but it is advisable to seek permission and to be accompanied. The Western visitor should bear in mind that mosques are essentially places for prayer and religious devotion. Yemenis are proud of their mosques, but regard architectural magnificence as secondary to divine function.

Yemen has three of the most ancient mosques in the world, all founded during the lifetime of the Prophet. The Great Mosque in Sana'a is built on the site of the legendary twenty-storey Ghamdan Palace, and Sabaean columns have been incorporated into the present structure.

The mosque at Al Janad near Taiz has been rebuilt and restored on several occasions but still retains its aura of antiquity. The Great Mosque at Zabid achieved its definitive form during the golden age of the Rasulids in the 14th and 15th centuries. At that time the city of Zabid with its 230 Quranic schools was one of the leading Islamic universities.

Street scene in Zabid

The vestiges of Yemen's pre-Islamic past are geographically remote from today's centres of population. Marib is the most accessible. The new tarmac road from Sana'a permits comfortable day excursions. Baraqish demands a rough overland journey. Likewise a visit to the ancient capital of the Kingdom of Hadramaut at Shabwa requires some preparation. The final stage of the journey is a two-hour ride across open desert from the township of Atak on the fringe of the Empty Quarter. These trips are best undertaken with the co-operation of the tourism authorities or the Yemen Tourism Company. The remoteness of the sites heightens the appreciation of the old civilisations. The isolation of the archaeological remains helps to convey a much more direct experience of the past than would be possible amidst the constructions of modern development.

However, to view the cultural treasures of the old incense kingdoms the museums offer the best facilities. In Sana'a, the National Museum, and in Aden, the National Archaeological Museum, house unique collections of Himyaritic inscriptions, sculpture, and bas-relief which express the artistic achievements of Saba, Ma'in, Qataban, Ausan, Hadramaut and the Himyarites. Archaeologists, using scientific methods of excavation are bringing to light more and more evidence of Yemen's ancient history when the prosperity and culture of the region put south Arabia in the forefront of world civilisation.

Paradoxically, the recent past is more difficult to track down. The thousand-year Zaidi Imamate lasted until 1962, yet there are no mighty monuments which symbolise its glorious achievements. This is partly due to the curious nature of the Imamate itself. Founded essentially on religious inspiration rather than material or political ambition, the Zaidi system found its perfect expression in the person of the Imam. The empire-building fantasies usually associated with ruling elites are not to be found. Instead the vestiges of the Imamate are all personally connected with individual Imams. The countryside is dotted with the isolated and imposing structures of their palaces. Perhaps these symbols of defensive authority reveal the true nature of the Zaidi period. The rule of the Imams was there for all to observe but never did it actually mould the essential fabric of Yemeni life in its own image. The palaces resemble outposts of some distant power seeking to establish itself on foreign soil rather than as the direct expressions of native civilisation.

The dying days of the Imamate are powerfully present in Taiz, which Ahmad and Al Badr, the last of the Imams of Yemen, preferred to use as a capital. The palace is now a museum and displays the bric-a-brac and objects of finery collected from Europe and the Middle East with which the royal family surrounded itself. Things have been left much as they were in 1962. Bottles of French perfume, rows of Swiss watches, and toys from London gather dust. The discordant mass of imported luxuries leaves a vivid impression of the gulf which had opened between the fantasy world of the last of the Imams and the grim reality of the life of the Yemeni populace.

Remains of the British colonial period in Aden and the Protectorate are still in evidence. The distinctive red pillar boxes are somewhat incongruous in the surroundings of the Hadramaut, but no-one appears to mind them. Aden itself is full of reminders of the British time. There has been little attempt to cover up the old imperial connection. The miniature replica of Big Ben on Steamer Point has fallen victim to neglect rather than to any instinct for demolition. Similarly, the Crescent Hotel has not received the investment necessary for its upkeep. Money is channelled into new projects rather than in the restoration of older properties.

However, there are definite signs that a change in policy has taken place. Both the Yemen Arab Republic and the People's Democratic Republic of Yemen are now committed to the joint development of tourism and the related infrastructure. The founding of the Yemen Tourism Company in 1981 as an independent commercial organisation with private as well as state financing is a symbol of this intention. The YTC has a variety of functions which cover the promotion and marketing of tourism for both Yemens as well as providing tour facilities and running a chain of traditional Yemeni-style hotels. Furthermore, the YTC, through its key role in developing domestic tourism between North and South, is pioneering freedom of movement which is a prior condition to political union.

Air transport is making considerable progress. Sana'a serves as the home base of Yemenia, which maintains direct international services to Europe, India and the Middle East. Most visitors to Yemen presently arrive at Sana'a International Airport and proceed with Yemenia to Taiz, Sa'da, or Hodeidah. Aden, home of Al Yemda, provides access to Mukalla and the cities of the Hadramaut.

Ground transport between the principal cities is cheapest by collective taxi but more comfort is to be had by hiring a private taxi. Small groups tend to travel in four-wheel drive vehicles with driver provided by such travel operators as Yemen Tourism Company in Sana'a and Arabia Felix Tourist in Aden. The cost of reliable transport with experienced driver is worthwhile and gives the visitor more freedom to explore remote places.

Although both Yemens are constituted as Islamic Republics and observe Quranic principles there is no ban on alcoholic drinks in the main hotels. This tolerance is part of the Yemeni tradition but should not be mistaken for a laxness of attitude. In most respects Yemenis are extremely conservative and modest in social behaviour.

Street market in Sana'a

The country is often called a time capsule, even a museum, because the past is still so much alive and functioning. Yet there are signs of profound shifts under way as a result of the economic boom fuelled by the oil revenues of the neighbouring states of the Arabian peninsula. Although Yemen is yet to join the league of oil producers, it has been drawn into the nexus of the petro-dollar age. Perhaps as many as 500,000 Yemenis are working in Saudi Arabia alone. The remittance money of the expatriates is a welcome boost to the Yemeni economy but its effect is highly inflationary. More serious is the absence of so many skilled workers who are vitally necessary to build up the basis of national development. Agriculture, the traditional mainstay of the country which employs eighty per cent of the population, is being quite literally eroded by rival opportunities in neighbouring states. Increased cultivation of *qat* is reducing the output of locally grown food and thereby creating a dependence on imported produce.

Nevertheless, agriculture remains the brightest long-term prospect for Yemen. The high mountains which catch the south-west monsoon provide a unique environment within the Arabian peninsula. Coffee, sorghum, cotton, papaya, grapes and tobacco are some of the wide range of crops which thrive in Yemen. Yemenis can console themselves with the thought they can still be self-sufficient in food long after their oil-rich neighbours have exhausted their oil reserves. Certainly, the temperate climate of the central highlands of Yemen is a major asset which will provide a means of survival whatever happens to the economy.

Tourism is seen as an important means of earning foreign exchange but there is considerable awareness of the dangers which too much tourism might bring. Yemen is lucky to be able to benefit from the hard lessons of other countries whose cultures have been undermined by an excess of marketing zeal. However, in a sense Yemen is protected from the adverse effects of mass tourism by the very nature of its attractions. Culture and climate are the two magnets which draw visitors. The country is ideally suited to small groups of interested individuals, keen to discover the unique archaeological and architectural heritage of a forgotten corner of the world's civilisation.

Yemen has always been a mystery to the outside world. Even during the boom millennium of the incense trade the Greeks and Romans knew little about the country. In more recent centuries the instinctive distrust of the Imams and the well-nigh impenetrable nature of the terrain have conspired to keep foreigners at a distance. Over the past decade the veil of secrecy has been lifted so that Yemen is now easily accessible to travellers. It is timely to remember the words of the much quoted but anonymous Persian scholar: "Yemen must be seen, even if the journey is long."

Modern air transportation has brought Yemen within seven hours of Europe. The rediscovery of Yemen, once at the crossroads of East-West trade routes and cradle of Arabian culture, is now one of those last frontiers to be opened to the travellers of the world. The journey there might not be long but ample time should be allowed to visit the country. Yemen is more than the sum of its monuments and scenery. A civilisation which is at least three thousand years old offers many layers of reality. Only the relaxed traveller will be able to let the Yemen experience work its full magic.

Selected Further Reading

BIDWELL, ROBIN *The Two Yemens*, Longman, London 1983

COSTA, PAOLO & VICARIO, E. *Yemen: Land of Builders*, Academy edns, London 1978

DOE, BRIAN *Southern Arabia*, Thames and Hudson, London 1971

GROOM, NIGEL *Frankincense and Myrrh*, Longman, London 1981

INGRAMS, HAROLD *Arabia and the Isles*, John Murray, London 1942

MACRO, ERIC *Yemen and the Western World since 1571*, Hurst, London 1968

NIEBUHR, CARSTEN *Travels through Arabia*, Edinburgh 1792, reprinted Beirut 1968

SERJEANT, R. B. & LEWCOCK, RONALD *Sana'a – An Arabian Islamic City*, Scorpion Press, World of Islam Festival Trust, London 1983

STARK, FREYA *The Southern Gates of Arabia*, John Murray, London 1942

STOOKEY, ROBERT *Yemen: the Politics of the Yemen Arab Republic*, Westview, Boulder, California 1978

South Yemen, Westview, Boulder, California 1982

WISSMAN, HERMAN VON & VAN DER MEULEN, D. *The Hadramaut – Some of its Mysteries Unveiled*, Leyden 1933, reprinted Brill, Leyden 1964

Index

158